The Rusty Pumpkin

Edited by Nicholas Kistler

Introduction by William Thomas

Cover Design by Mariella Story

Instagram: @Mariella.Story

Website:

https://mariellastory.wixsite.com/fineartist

The Rusty Pumpkin

October, 2023

The Wheel Collective LLC

Boulder, Colorado 80301 U.S.A.

"I am so glad I live in a world where there are Octobers"

-L.M. Montgomery

<u>Contributors</u>

<u>(And IG handles/websites)</u>

Mariella Story

@Mariella.Story

William Thomas

@river_mann_band

Audrey Houghton

@whatalovelyyday

Alex Schwartzberg

@_powerpuffsquirrel

Indica Gaess

@indiroseartistry

Nicholas Kistler

@beardyspiritualman

Johanna Hernandez

lyramagdalene@gmail.com

James Tien

@bearpawzmt & @Shepherd_of_thefield

Zach Horvitz

Kabbalisticimaginarium.carrd.co

Sky Urspruch

Zak Reinhart

@zakreinhart

Ryan Nash

@sitwithryan

Mila Womb

Huck Shine

Darkleaf.org & @darkleafpublicatio

The Pivot: A Cross-Quarterly Collection

The Wheel Collective is excited to share the first of what we hope to be a series of publications called The Pivot. This series is an active investigation into how the arts can help us better resonate with the cycles of nature and the turning of the Wheel of the Year. As a central theme in most if not all the world's wisdom traditions, the human relationship to the seasonality and cycles implicit in natural process is an evolutionary and, potentially, revolutionary endeavor.

Our roots are in seasonality, as is our inevitable future. Thus, we must do what all great peoples have done to one extent or another. We must consciously investigate our physical, psychological, and spiritual relationship to season and the change that is its imperative and its essence.

We can make of our art (that which we cannot help but do) our investigation; our prayer and participation in the process of constant relation, the cycles of which we make sense of in seasons. We can make of our art an exploration into those very seasons themselves. Whether it is building a spiral in the town square on the winter solstice or journaling when the chi of the early morning is in resonance with the colon; the artistic act informs us constantly regarding where we sit in time and with what we are resonating.

We can use this insight to begin to grasp a more complete picture of our role, and possible redemption, as members of the wider community of life on this planet and its associated worlds. Learning that we may write more about our mother in September and more about our fears in deep winter, that we tend to like this kind of music in the morning, and prefer this kind of book at night; even those little insights begin to establish a more tangible context.

This is a fundamentally mythic context and makes use of personal association and analogical reasoning to make relevant the symbols and essences that define the points on the Wheel of the

Year. Most simply these points are represented by the solstices, equinoxes, and cross-quarter days (Imbolc, Beltane, Lammas, and Samhain). These days serve as pivots at which we can recognize the aspects of season that are fundamental to the turnings of change. There is much to be said about the dynamic between human and season and much wisdom to be gleaned from the exploration of this synthesis. For our purposes, however, we will keep things vague.

At present our emphasis is on the Cross Quarter days, largely because at least one of our members thought the cross-quarter days would be somewhat delightful to publish on and the rest of us agreed!

If the solstices are the extremity and the equinoxes are the mid-points, then the cross-quarter days are equidistance from both midpoint and extremity. It could be said that they sit in the middle of motion. They are dynamic and rooted in processes as opposed to states. It should be noted here, for the sake of clarity, that when we discuss the Wheel of the Year we are inevitably also speaking of the cycle of Birth, Death and inevitable Resurrection.

Each of the cross-quarter days represents a moment in that endless process that has been frozen out of nematic necessity.

Imbolc marks the end of winter and the time for preparing the fields for crops. We know it as Groundhog Day and it is the point where life decides, so kindly, to return as fully as the spectacle of Spring.

Lammas marks the harvest and holds the initial turning toward old-age (and wisdom) that follows the total maturation of high Summer.

Beltane is the time to take the herds to higher pastures and when young cattle and sheep are to be weaned, it is connected to generation, fertility, birth and a sense of sprouts and initial blossoming.

To complete the circle, Samhain is, in a sense, when the cows come home (and the spirits come close behind). It is All Saints Day and its eve, Halloween, is when the veil between worlds is the thinnest. It is both decay and dying, the initiation of Scorpio.

It marks the plunge into winter, the initiation of the descent into the Womb Tomb of the great mother. It is a marker of decay and refinement, leading to the catalytic death that initiates rebirth. To the artist it is pertinently Orpheus' descent into the underworld. When we cross the thinning veil into our unconscious on the quest, with the new self-context we have gained through the cycle, to reclaim the muse.

Long story short, we are pleased as punch to present a seasonal periodical that explores the dynamic interplay of the seasons with the effulgent nature of the human spirit.

For this, our first edition, we have compiled a litany of pieces from local boulder artists and writers that deal, if only tangentially, with the seasonal energies of Samhain.

Without further ado we are thrilled to present to you the first edition of The Pivot.

-*William Thomas*

The Rusty Pumpkin

A Note from a Grateful Editor

I am inordinately pleased to present the first edition of The Wheel Collective's quarterly periodical, *The Pivot no.1: The Rusty Pumpkin.*

With submissions from singers, songwriters, teachers, writers, visual artists, choreographers, meditation teachers, and a host of other interesting persons; I want to note the absolute pleasure that it has been sifting through all the submissions that we've received. I have immensely enjoyed reading each and every one of them.

The arts are a fickle thing, and it has been my experienced that even among the most talented artists and writers, it is all too common to be almost completely unknown to a wider audience other than the immediate friends and family that we hold hostage to our creativity.

In that vein it brings me tremendous pleasure to showcase the work of some immensely talented and interesting individuals in the hopes that others among us on this big blue rock called earth might be moved by the work of these exceptionally wonderful individuals, as I have been.

There is a ton of folks that need thanking for making this quarterly possible, not the least of which is the entire core Wheel Team; you know who you are and I love you.

I also want to thank all of the wonderful folks who submitted and whose work is what makes something like this tangible.

Last but not least, I want to thank you, whoever is reading this right now.

Because of your support, small collectives, and publications like this one can print periodicals, host events, help folks run workshops and classes, and just generally make things more interesting.

On behalf of all our artists and The Wheel Team, thank you from the bottom of my heart.

-Nick

A Dedication

May all beings be redeemed in the light of their true nature. May they be free from the bondage of false myth and may they laugh readily and often. May it be that all people can cry when it is time to grieve, and sing and dance whenever possible. May each being practice their art daily and for its own sake.

A Prayer of Gratitude

Gratitude to the spirits of the land we walk on.

Gratitude to the halls of mind we wander through.

Gratitude to the soul we breath with.

Gratitude to the Seasons for teaching us how to breath

Gratitude to the Earth, our only home and mother.

Gratitude to the ancestors and lineage that stand behind these artists and their work.

Gratitude to humanity and its perfectly divine madness.

The Poetry of James Tien

Messenger

Like the Sun
which never retires in its work,
each day faithful to shine,
Arising from a place of no disturbance,
and settling in a land without beginning,
the voice of a cock's groaning,
and settling in its motion
another image left behind,
hastening to follow and unable to catch up,
pouring a lasting drop into a fountain
without a dry season

The Bear (*Spring*)

A large relaxed body
a solid frame to support it.
Extending down and out, rooting,
reaching paws up, the sides outstretched
Yawning a breath of happy joy
reverberating on the forest floor
licking the lips-and savoring the taste
already in the mouth
Deep satisfying growls from the furnace of
the belly
as the weight is carried with distinguished
grace,
The hips and back command respect,
the sense gates are wide and far-reaching,
The mind synced up with the pulse of
nature,
from long sitting in hibernation,
ready to wake again and smell the flowers

The Bear (*Fall*)

The last of summer's flower's fragrance
fading off the tip of the nose
fallen berries under my paw so hairy
under winter's coat my back is buried
Cold breeze blowing me home
All fours on the forest floor
Whence I stood
leaves hide to reveal the wood
A belly fat and full of feasting
My weight carries me while i'm resting
Like a dead man
I do nothing while digesting
I close my eyes
The body hides
My likeness appears in the skies
In inner chambers my warmth is kept
breathing naught but the smell of breath
Warmly passing over my tongue
through spaces between the teeth
How do I hold on to heat?
Now asleep I feed the dream with the last
meal I eat
until next Spring
when I'll be catching Salmon

The Poetry of William Thomas

CROSSDANCER

In the quiet between the wind and the
laughter of a mountain stream
there was just audible the sound of an owl
chuckling at the moonlight.
She danced there tangibly, effervescent,
clean
wearing nothing but her own scandal
the body of reflected light that ever calls to
me.

She was a dancer and I cursed myself for
that,
She was quiet and I lay out wretched as I
waited for her
to answer me in a language I knew, a
language of lyric
not merely of tongue and flesh and flame.
I know her not by a name, but by a memory
of sense
by the scent of moonlight on water and by
her hair

that is crystal and silver and black as the
night
I know her as "double-sided-coin-of-my-
body"
of my body's memory, its grand allegory of
sensation
that taught Kings to be noble and Maiden's
to bleed.

Adonis cries, and cries and cries for
something else
for anything that is not this wretched thigh
wound
this wound of
 sacrament and savagery, sanctimony
and the boar tusked woman drinks his tears
takes them like memory in the shade of
aspen
weaving them inside her lungs and singing
their melody
singing it into the world of things and into
majesty.
That song of Tears and temperature of
tongue
Has caste the chaste condition of my infamy
And I still walk adonis on a leash in the
stable
Because Crossdancer told me I was already
free

A Body and Two Rivers

The body of the mother is heaving,
the unconscious in all her silver and glory
is out of breath and shaking.
Every moment
every lived out lie to time
when we cannot confess
and we cannot control
these moments of in-between
when I see but can't go
and all those tired eyes lay wanting...

                    —those moments scare me.

Do you confuse yourself with emblem
myth, mirth, and majesty
do you satiate symbol
giving them treats of your flesh
so you can feel worthy
because you must feel worthy
you must feel seen
and heard and listened to,
you should even feel loved.

But when the dark comes in
and the only ones there
to see you suffer

are all the symbols you used
to build yourself a ladder
so you could remain so very far
from the plague that is your flesh.
Those symbols listen
 to your pained cries
they listen,
they speak back to you,
they mumble
little things to be and think and wear
to smoke and drink and masturbate to,
they speak back in unconscious context
in a memory that lives in your skin
and makes you more likely
to suck somebody's dick without meaning
to.
Symbol becomes habit, I think,
and it must then be us
that will heal our relationship
to symbol,
together
breathing our bodies beside one another.
From wanting sex and image
to choose life and deity

I think I need you on this long walk
and I think you need me too
I think if we alternate carrying different
bags

we wont get tired in the same muscles so
quickly
and if you carry the water you can be
Charon
in my dreams when we sleep by canyon
light
you will be ancient and not unkind
you will be the Water Man
and I will carry the lantern when we must
continue
up a bluff in dark for fear of injury, and of
trespass.
I will carry the lantern and be glad to
consume you
by mirror of some hand outstretched
out of shadow and darkness' memory
I will make light from your mystery
burning the water perfectly
I will make your ripples bold
tie semblance to your infamy
and cry out only half your name
before the mind of Limen
stretches out its memory
to hold me in my flesh
as I cross excarnal beds
of two great rivers
one of love
and one of death.

<u>More Than Mind</u>

I usually save my poetic orgasms for
gallbladder time,
between 1 am and 3 am
when the weather of what is to come
is easily wasted

but chemicals make even morning
something fatty to be processed
and if you pretend that you
could be solely liver a time
solely anger without transgression
(that you do not call anger
that you call fancy, and demon
water and devil and mind),
if you could be anger
and also remember yourself
would you still sit here writing
as if to somehow set it free?

but mind is more than mind,
much more than anger is springtime and
the tragedy of circumstance
was written in a web of time
by a spider with a thousand names.

these bodies are like dew drops

impermanent and necessary,
they make the morning soluble
so the kidneys can dream
their dream that is not
a dream, that is nothing
but the way we must make sense
of the welcome anticipation
that is the revolt of a soul
in the face of a system
that is its own crucible.
that system, its own disaster and madness,
inevitably its own salvation,
binding, Alkhemet.

Shower Song

If light were alone to bare the weight
of all that comes with dreaming,
would it defile the halls of clay
to know its own eyes gleaming?
Or would it simply cast around
forgetting love was made by sound
until the moment that it found
God's answer was his singing?

A Visual Interlude
The Art of
Audrey Houghton

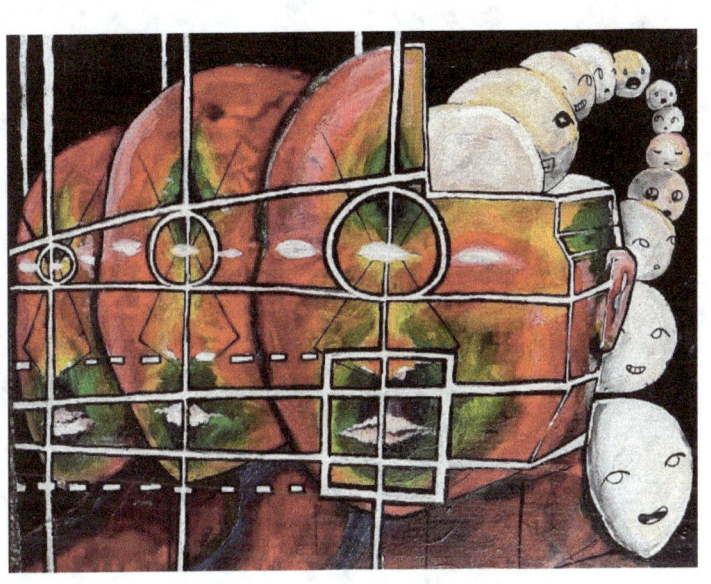

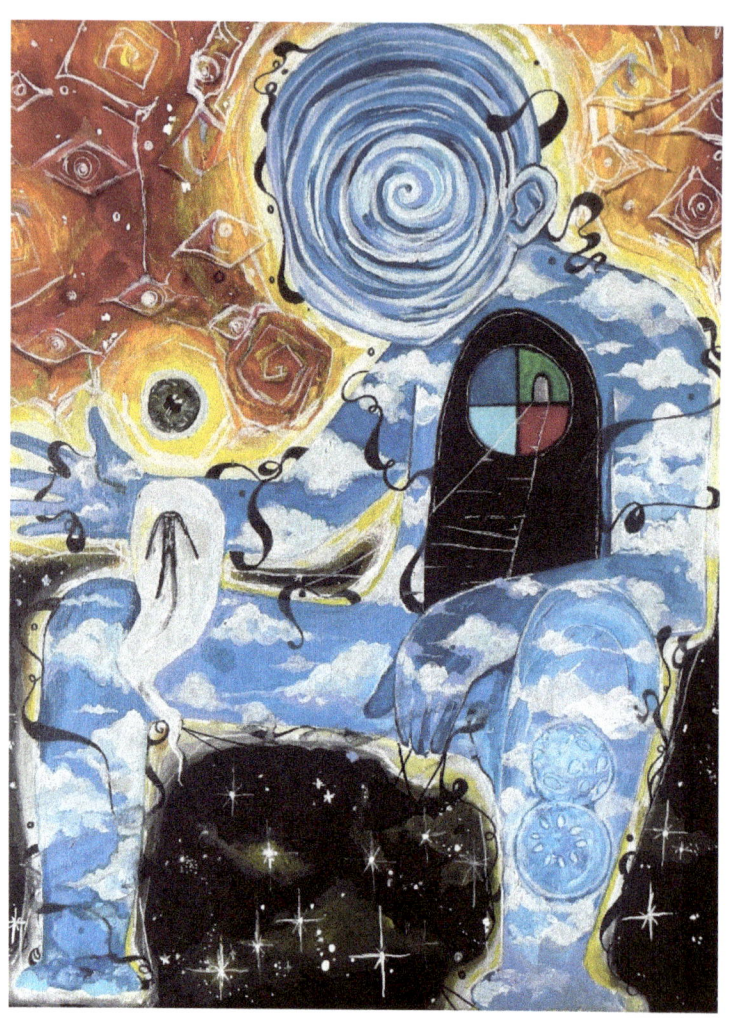

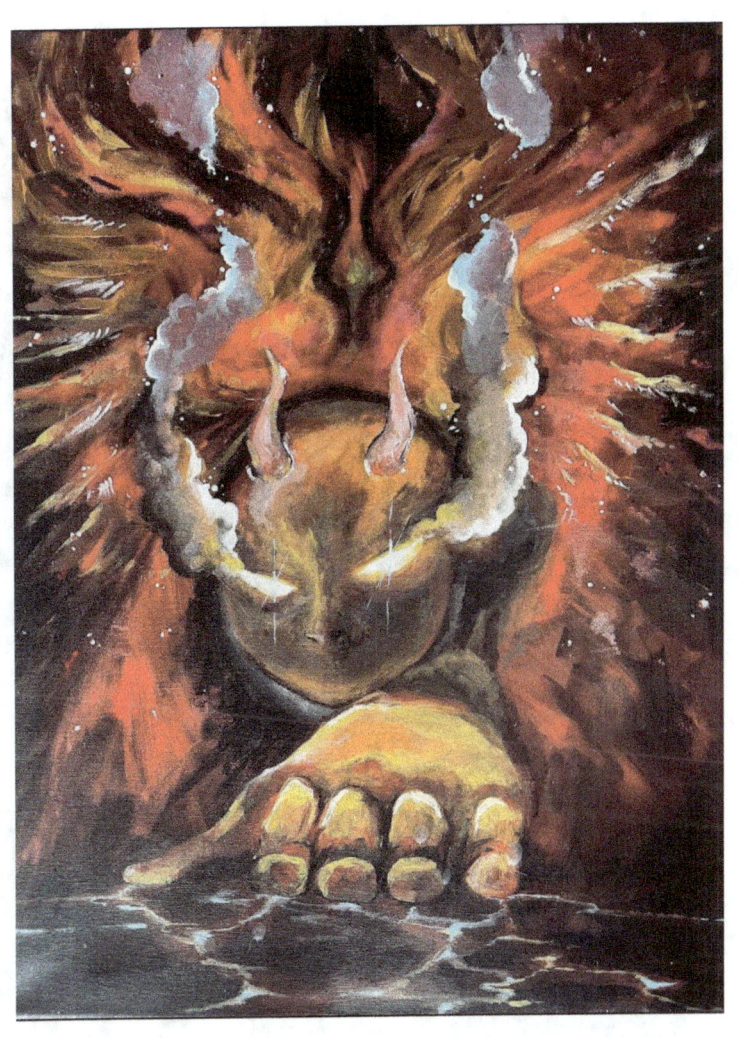

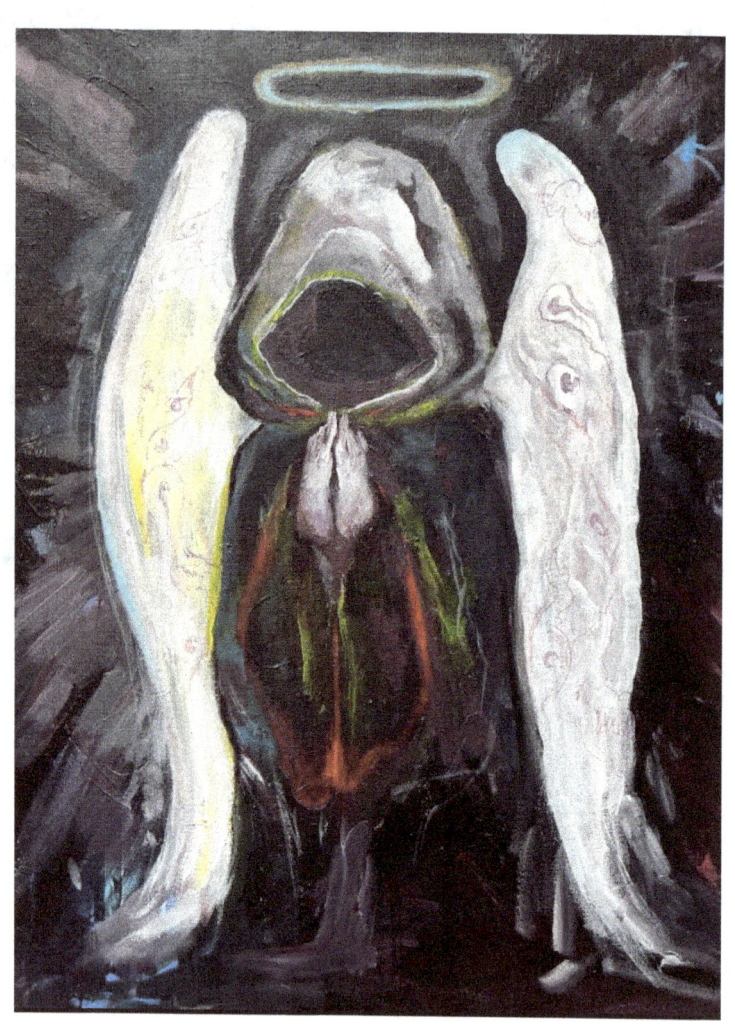

The Poetry of Zach Horvitz

SWANSONG OF THE ETERNAL SOLDIER

I died in the Onin War, under cherry
blossoms, I died in Mongolia, under the rule
of Khan, (arms
lopped off like goat-legs for soup.) I died
in France, before Paris was liberated
(from the Swastika banner and the
intoxicated forces beneath it, meth-heads
and war-drunk foes...) Neither De Gaulle
nor God
gave me medal, nor place amid celestial
thrones. I died with the divine wind; I was
the divine wind, once. I fought on both
sides
of the same battle, before I knew who I was.
I bifurcated my soul
and found myself on two different fronts, I
puked
in two different trenches, I fought

with katana and rifle, with sabre and shield;
fought with firecracker, before the green
grenade; with physics, before and after the
bomb (to reconcile
the many and the one, to resolve the
dialectic of history,) before and after
Idealism and the owl
of Minerva flying at dusk. Endlessly
I died; and again
I am dying — a different death. I
am dying the death of the spirit, because in
America you kill kin for sport, (like a game,
a gladiator game.) In your schools. In your
streets,
your houses
of worship, you take up arms against
yourselves. You take life from the dream for
which I gave my life, life after life.

SELF-EXILE FROM MY ELYSIUM

When I think of the Elysian Fields
I never imagine Greek farmland
or Achilles with laurels of gold and green.
I always imagine Provence at dusk,
full of purple, next to the outdoor pool
where the dead horseman used to swim
naked in front of everyone — not only
in front of his lover or the child for whom
innocence and shame were not yet words.
That was the purest place I don't want
to return to — because I fear a homecoming
would either be too perfect to withstand,
or else those fields of abundant lavender
would be nothing special at all.

BECOMING COMBUSTIBLE

It is said that when the Heart Sutra was first
spoken, some vomited, and many hearts
exploded.
The Elohim told Moses, "None shall see my
face and live."
When the aliens invade,
who will be able to behold
with their own eyes
those dazzling ships?
There are sparks of wisdom
too lofty for the ears, for the body to
contain, without becoming combustible, like
a tiny
cosmos, in the presence of
a greater cosmos, swallowed.

Encounters with the Gods
By Sky Urspruch

Imagine you're lost in a museum. You can't figure out how you got in, how to exit out, or what kind of museum it even is, but you accept not knowing and take a stroll. Strange art adorns the walls: paintings in dark minor keys, statues of gaunt boned men…

Okay, odd, but you keep strolling on. Around the corner a massive painting stretches across

the far wall, glowing in splendid oilish light. You walk up to it and see that the figure inside the frame moving – she's moving. She towers over you! Tall as a redwood and as wide as the sea. Her eyes pierce you, unveil you: the years you've gained are washed away. The frame evaporates, the museum with it, and all that's left is you and her. But

you're not staring like a tourist anymore, no. It's as if her beauteous forms, her dimension, her entire being is somehow connected to your raw attention. This isn't your first time with her. You know that you've relied on her all of your life: on her presence, her feelings. You've felt her in times of bliss and wonder as the shiver on the nape of your neck. You're her child, but with no taint of helplessness, no crutch of dependence. You are born of her as she is spirited through you.

You ask for her name, but you know immediately. She's Isis, yes, or Venus perhaps, but even more she's… She's the faerie mother from the story time circles. You never needed to look farther than the fairytales to find her.

This is what encountering the many Gods is like for me. The museum is my mind at the frontier of the unknown. The enormous painting is the doorway to the deity. The encounter with the Goddess of Love is emblematic of the experience of inner contact: there's the initial fright as you pass over the threshold, followed by a burst of joy and beauty, followed then by a remembrance; one that bridges the wisdom of the body to the wisdom of things past, flowing out into my future hopes and dreams.

There is an endless series of deities accessible to the modern practitioner, but my own practice tends to focus on the seven deities that correspond to the seven classical planets of the solar system.

There's the lord of the Sun: Ra, Helios, Apollo. It's in the solar god that I see the lord of this earthbound universe: the primary source of light, self-luminous, wise, and bright. It's through his light that the spectrum of colors originates, and therefore all other gods find their resolution in him. The sun is raw power, and his avatars shed light without thought of who is worthy of it. He is the ultimate edge that major keys have over their minor counterparts, the absolute triumph of consciousness in a dark and chaotic universe.

Ever alongside the Solar God is his lunar partner in the Moon: Isis, Artemis, Persephone, Hekate, and the mysterious Triple Goddess are all favorite avatars of mine.

Also, in the moon I see Ganesha, Thoth, and other lords of magic and initiation. Unlike the Sun the Moon is not self-luminous, but its avatars are much closer to the human. The Moon holds the reins over the oceans, over the tides of our lives. It is also to the Moon that artists howl too, and which poets sing to. Within the moon is a mutable beauty which reflects the source in the same way that a blank canvas reflects the painter, or that a theater receives a singer or actor. Whereas the sun is the source of magic and fantasy, the moon is them in our hands.

Then there's the quicksilver planet Mercury: Hermes, Thoth (yes, Thoth again, none of this is 1:1), and all the trickster deities from Loki to the Coyote. On one hand Mercury is a trickster, a liar, a salesman and a thief. On the other Mercury is the closest friend and servant of the Sun. He is all wit, humor, hilarious hijynx, who nevertheless holds the secrets of the high arts and sciences. He's the patron deity of writers, merchants, travelers, even politicians; of anybody who wishes to bend reality with their words.

Mercury is also a nerd, a theoretician in need of a girlfriend, who seriously needs to shut the fuck up and listen.

Venus needs little introduction. Whereas the Moon is more the wise and

independent sister, Venus is the forever girlfriend and lover (and the admittedly Oedipal mother). She is warm, receptive, flowing, constant and bright. If the Moon is the distant muse, then Venus is the muse who never leaves my arms. She is the utter ecstasy of

sex, of art-making, of love in all kinds. She's embodied in the Aphrodite of the Greeks, in

Egypt as Hathor, but most of all in the beloved soul-spouse of all true lovers.

Mars, Ares, the god of war and vengeance as also embodied by Thor. Mars is the patron spirit of the warrior who fights within and without. He represents the tougher sides of life. You can see him in weaponry, in iron discipline. Martial arts are named after him. He's the god that nobody likes but who demands respect. Nowadays Mars is most embodied by the football coach, the martial arts instructor, and the drill sergeant.

Less obviously, he's embodied by anyone who won't give up on their dream.

In contrast to Mars is Jupiter: old Jove, the good father, the wise and just lord of the peace. In a way Old Jove is God the Father in his most beneficial aspect: the fatherly blessing that tells his children they are loved and are capable of journeying out into their highest selves. In The Rolling Stones song "Shine a Light" the chorus goes: "May the good lord shine a light on you!" – That's the message that Jove sends. Jupiter is the redemption of the father from centuries of vague restriction and command.

At the edge of the solar system is Saturn, Kronos. He is the oldest of the gods and the… Least personable. The ancient belief is that Saturn is the gatekeeper of our universe, keeping things out and basically keeping us all trapped within…

Nevertheless, Saturn should not be feared, for beneath his dour exterior is the primordial wisdom of the most ancient of days. Whereas all the other gods are bright and energetic, Saturn is cold, dry, heavy and dark. This is for the best though, because Saturn helps me recall the force of matter in relation to spirit. The Hermetic axiom goes: as above so below.

All the spiritual insight in the world means nothing if I can't make peace with the most bitter facts of the material world. Therefore, Saturn is also the god of death: the messenger of the dark truth that paradoxically brings me deeper into the life I know I have. Saturn helps me get my shit together.

I worship the planetary deities because no matter how far out they get conceptually, they are each grounded within the physical universe, within colossal sources of matter and energy that have enchanted the human minds since the dawn of days. Whether they're interpreted as seven individual deities, or seven deities that are aspects of one single deity is a matter left up to the worshipper. What matters to me is that they're all gods that I can feel through me, no matter where I am.

The king, the magician, the writer, lover, warrior, the ancient one, my holy mother, my holy father... I know them all as parts of myself. When I bring myself to contact one, the six others are elucidated by contrast.

It all informs a sense of vastness and divinity without and within.

The Poetry of Johanna Hernandez

Slain God

the cusp of all Time
lays suspended on that axis of
the one slain and resurrected God.

He who is murdered, crucified, burned,
and buried.

and either fallen for the love of an
ungrateful people,
or suspect to the atrocious hands of Fate,
to the Underworld, He goes.

thus, the Lady's chalice
shall remain forever unfilled.
until, like the ever-dying sun,
He rises like a phoenix in the heavens.

then, in love and peace, the world shall
spin....
Dizzy.

spinning....
Spun.

until the leaves of fall start to drift to the
ground,
and the circle will renew,
and bite its own tail.

<u>September Thoughts</u>

Seasons change.
Light to dark, death and life.
We all face the slow onset of time and
we are all reborn in the Spring.
Except people who pick their noses in the
car.
You think I can't see you?
Your windows are *glass*.
That's nasty.

A Visual Interlude
The Art and Words of
Alex Schwartzberg

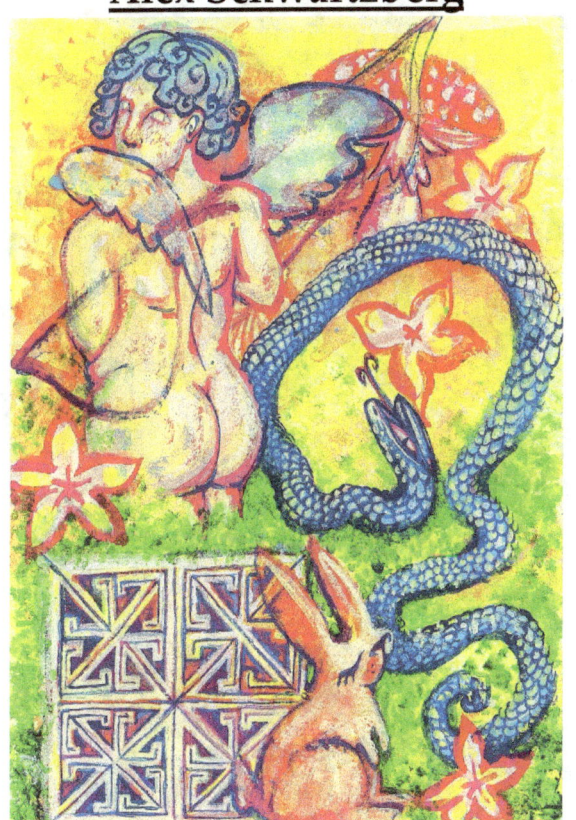

Ego Death

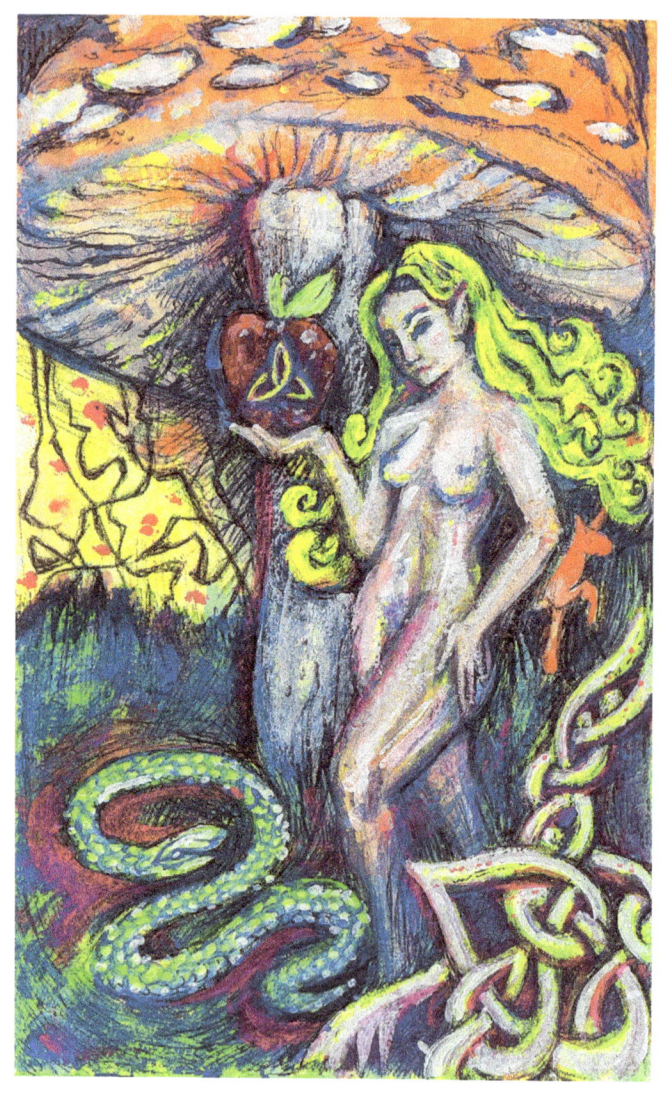

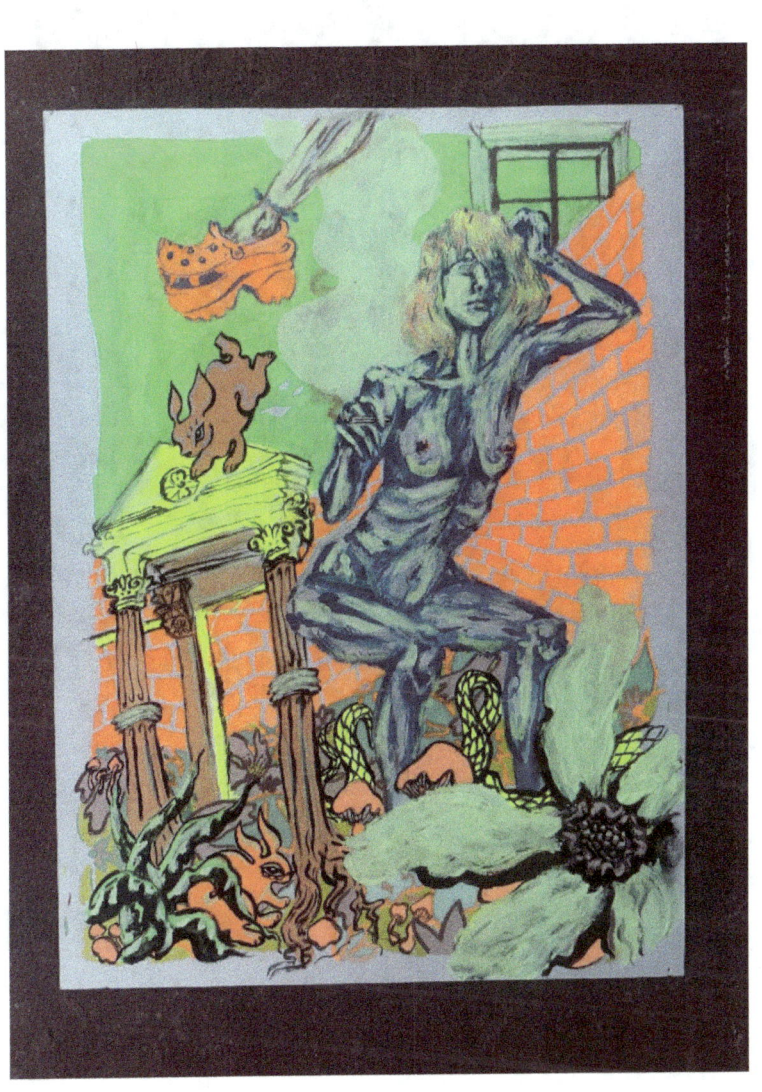

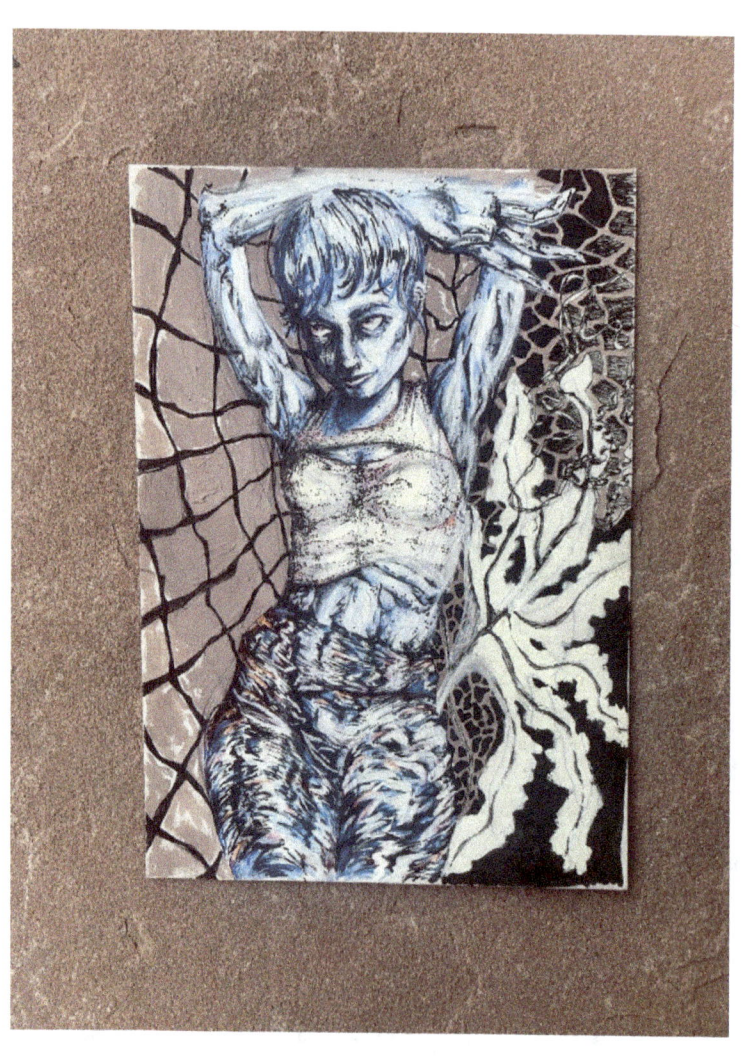

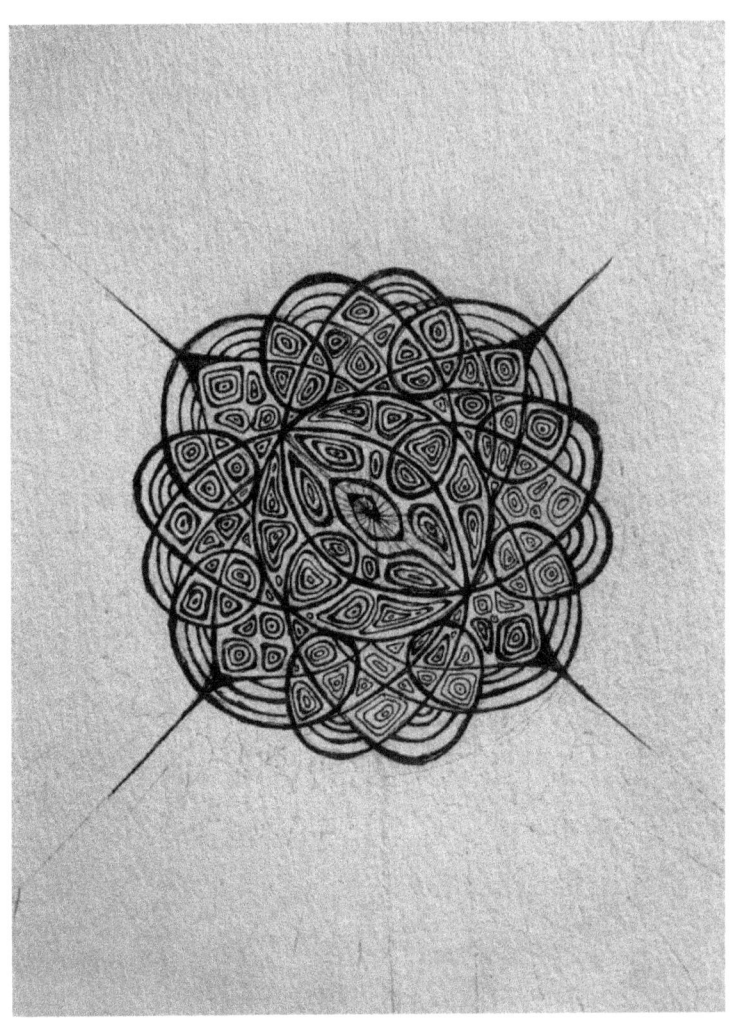

Words for Images

Ouroboros…
was a dog:
Pandora/Eve
A woman of clay, forged in the image of a
Goddess.
A plaything for mankind.
They shaped her into a spider,
She drank the blood of the "wicked" to
serve
and protect the "Righteous Gods".
She broke free and ran to the forested
coastline, back to the Ocean.
Back to the clay source,
Mother Earth:
Ancestor of all of our Ancestors.
Inside a the belly of a cave,
she found her seal skin.
She could once again sing to Poseidon.
Protected by an ancient and new
technology:
Presence.
Now here we are
Laying still, awaiting the next wave to
blanket this tiny portion of shoreline.
Exhaustion and then peace.
Ultimate release…Ouroboros

The Poetry of Indica Gaess

Crows Nest

[sacred space, sacred space
from father to daughter; a tradition, a
birthplace]

A Sherpa; I guide us
up winding mountain dirt roads
curves carved so deep
(they dwell in my hip-bones)
past sunshine slopes and those well to-do
content in silence, just me and you

we pull off to admire the master at work
zipping coats, sipping tea, packing snacks,
switching shirts
and as he pulls his lengthy rays back east
with steady hand settles,
soothes
the beasts

setting off on our journey, we thank le Soleil
waving
and continue up the rocky driveway

as he gently tucks in both friends and foe
with his (steadily) fading evening glow

peering upwards through slow-moving
gloom
I watch a cloud near swallow(s)— Oh!
it's la Lune!
taking the stage for her act of the day
eyes twinkling
catching humans at play

she blushes, her cheeks the palest pink
yet seems to grow instead of shrink
result of Chinook's late-night caress
(I can feel him leaning
over top of crows nest)

her rosy glow casts far and wide
even softening the features of stern Mr.
Divide
he comes to rest,
his frame grounded in presence
And gently reminds me of my own
evanescence

[sacred space, sacred space
from father to daughter; a tradition, a
birthplace]

If I could peel my heart
Blood orange
Prepackaged for the giving
Rind thick meat raw
And place a small section
Atop the gentle tongue
Of each soul i adore

That, i think,
Would be the physical act of poetry

My Miraculous Capacity to Believe my Own Bullshit
By Nicholas Kistler

My miraculous capacity to believe my own bullshit is only rivaled by my propensity for self-indulgence. The thing about the whole spiritual trip is, most of us won't even bother with it unless we feel like we're going to get something out of it.

The crutch of being human seems that we never really do anything unless we're promised some sort of result, some payoff;' lower blood pressure, access to hot yoga babes, an imperturbable sense of inner peace; or, if we think rather highly of ourselves, a fleeting glimpse of eternity.

But let's not mistake aspiration for motivation. No matter how "noble" our goal, it's a results-oriented mindset all the way down.

And that's just as well. If that's what it takes to get our glutes on the cushion of transcendence, so be it.

The longer we yearn for something other than what's already going on, the more we start to realize that no matter how hard we try, or how long we meditate, no matter how many initiations we get our grubby mits on, no matter how many swamis we sit at the feet of who promise us enlightenment at the end of *this* blowjob, we're not actually going anywhere.

We're never going to get any closer in the pursuit of this whole idea of enlightenment because, truth be told, you can't attain enlightenment.

There's nothing to attain to.

The notion that we can obtain some transcendent state of being belies the fact that we think that we're actually somebody due for something that isn't already voluminously present.

We've been had!

And the more we cling, or strive, or crave for the results-oriented approach to spiritual gains, *the more we want it,* the more it's going to slip through our fingers like sand through our sweaty hands.

In a sick twist, our desire for reality obscures it's true nature.

The longer that we think we're somebody, doing something, the harder it is to get it!

If we're angling for enlightenment and we're really trying to get free of the fetters of our unsightly personas or our family karma or our indigestion because we ate frozen waffles again for breakfast, the only way that we could hope to get extricated from our own nascent self-inflicted suffering is to surrender to the fact that we don't know dick about what's going on, the fact that anything at all is going on, *and that's OK*.

Nobody does.

But if we really cop to the fact that each and every moment is a mind-blowing symphony of shit we hardly understand, things get pretty strange.

Suddenly, external reality becomes an incredible show of color and wonder and the concept we call "I" is just doing itself.

Striving, or surrendering, or masturbating to pictures of Kim Kardashian, it's just doing its own thing.

It's only our own reflexive sense of self-importance that dares proclaim that any part of this magnificent process requires somebody behind the wheel.

What a blow to our sense of
individuality to concede that the miraculous
manifestation of reality doesn't require our
input in the slightest.

"I'm a meditator!"

"I'm a witch!"

"I'm unworthy!"

"I'm a follower of the blessed yogi Bear!"

Horse shit.

Awareness is already all pervading and
it defies any and all labels the knee jerk
reflex of consciousness so desperately wants
to attach to it.

At the end of the day, if we're very
lucky, we might come to the realization;
When it comes to liberation from our own
bullshit, there's nobody standing in the way
but us.

The Art of Mariella Story

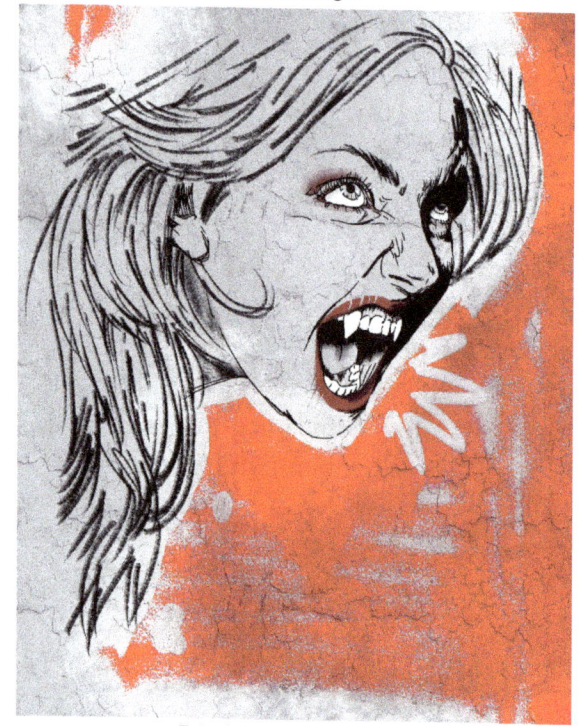

Living Dead Girl

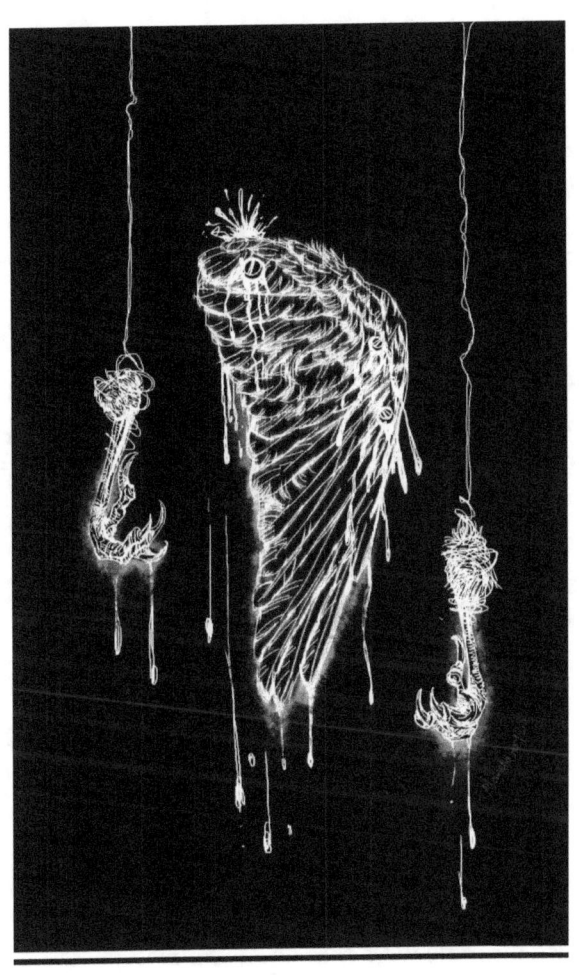

Crow Findings

The Poetry of Ryan Nash

Once upon a time,
Tap water was canned
and marketed as hardcore
Children rode electric motorcycles
and scared hobos shitless
Death sponsored them
as well as their company
Once upon a time
Beans were meat and meat were beans
To know less the difference meant innovation
And constipation a business opportunity

Once upon a time
Loitering was a felony
Sirens a symphony
Drug dealers had graduate degrees
and charged by the hour

Once upon a time
Mushrooms were more dangerous than
machine guns
And ska music made the only difference
Once upon a time
She was tight
He was hard

They were lollygagging
And we were so ready to turn it off but it was
made to keep us coming

Once upon a time
God took a big hit and so they made the box
Glass, tape, and vapes filled the space and so
we stayed

It became too much, we'd take a walk, then go
back to the box

That was the plot

Good Lama

Well, first offer it respect. If it spits on you
make sure to hold your composure and act as
if
nothing happened. There's a chance they
won't even know you're there, but maintain
the role of
indifference anyway. This is essential. You'll
also need them to be present, as they're
constantly
drifting, dissociating. So often it helps to yell
at them at the top of your lungs. But you want
to
stop just in time for their attention to come
online—any longer and they might fart
involuntarily
and kick you in the liver. In essence, you're
retrieving them, from themselves. And that's
not
always pretty. What you might find is that it
really doesn't like you. Again, it's essential to
not
take this personally. Remember, it might not
even know you're there if you're standing
right in
front of it. So don't read-in too hard. The key
is to meet them, draw them into
consciousness,

and share a moment of self-reflection. Make sure they know you're made of the same stuff. As you navigate this interplay, it might try to kick you again. A good trick is to yank on the 873rd

hair follicle near the withers. Nice and immediate...no hesitation, and umm...don't miss. If done

right, they'll release a subconsciously stored tribal yodel usually sung by one of their ancestors,

proceed to shake violently for a period, then black out and topple over from the intensity of the

experience. After a while though, they should get up and see you in a renewed light. An unshakable trust tends to be solidified at this point.

If you pull the wrong hair, well...let's not even go there.

WHAT I'VE FOUND IS

I'd like to unravel the cord that powers the
generator—
In wishing not
I in fact wish a lot
The one that feeds the meat that breathes and
sees into a world subsumed by a bunch of
meatings
In waiting for calm
I instead tie a knot
I want to trace these things back to their
origins but only with so much conviction
If I want to stop
why don't I check the clock?
Getting the rough idea is getting enough idea
as I'd otherwise have no room for error and
that's
where all the fun lies
I should then find
I'm utterly lost
We'd like to know what we are, but only to
the extent that we cannot know enough to
keep it
interesting
Know thy mess and be thy best
Know thy mess and be thy best
Wasn't there a book where the birds sang this
in synchrony?
More meat

The Enemy Wears
By Huck Shine

There is no confusion here as to who is the evil one in this battle. The evil one wears grey. I never look at him – not into his eyes. The one time I made that mistake, the truth became clear – the truth that he could see into me. He has told me that it's because we all wear white that he can 'read what's written on our blank faces' but I know the truth that he is the Devil. I saw the truth of that in his mirror black polished boots when he had me stripped and violated on my knees afront of him. His swirling red crown of flame and forked tongue waggling asky above my pathetic subservient and supine form below. I never knew how many faces I had until I saw myself in his reflective boots, and it was on that very day the voice came to me. That stormy Thursday, everything changed in this reality under that thunderous concrete sky.

"Officer Lemon" is what the others in grey were calling him. They were calling

50

out to him in fear and in anger. They obeyed his very whim. When he pointed – he pointed with all of his fingers extended as a blade – and where he pointed, those in grey would move and attack. Or -they would form a line. Or – they would deploy a demonic cloud of metal smoke upon us. That day, those in white were fighting back. Officer Lemon momentarily thought me to be a threat when he and his Demon Generals came upon me and he caught my eyes in his. Swift strike he had me in that web, reptilian seafoam green at center with no pupils and a broken mirror of red veins swirling - his sunken sockets bedded with black pillows. I knew then in that moment that he could see into me completely. He knew that I knew. Slowly I showed him the inside of my supplicant hands. He smiled slightly and showed me the force of the thunder above from the bottom of his boot with an explosive kick to the chest.

White cracked the sky.

As I slowly began to regain my knees, I could see the flames – orange and yellow and red in those polished hallways –

creating such a glorious spectacle. I could see silhouettes at war with a backdrop of curtained fire – smoke to catch the light in a fantastical haze… a fantastical and holy haze. Then I saw myself in his boots. Deep in that greytoned void I saw all of my selves. It was clear that he was speaking to me when I looked up to see his very human face in stark opposition to the visage of the hell god which had just been revealed to me in the truth of that spell. But I could only hear laughter, and I said but one word "Fire"

"Strip Convict!" came the very clear reply.

Same as always. Shame used against me; used against us. Everything is different now though. Now the voice tells me the future through his many mouths of the cracks in the walls here.

In my six by nine house – I wake, face to the cold hard floor. Haven't left this solitary cell in over a month now and I spend my days coming to know the soul that inhabits this place. I stay under the bunk, closest to the loudest crack I can find so as to communicate quietly – secretly. The voice of this prison prefers that I call him Master and I must admit to it feeling appropriate to our roles together. He tells me the future and I have promised Master my soul.

This-morning, through the slight black lightning shaped crack into the void in the corner, Master told me that I will kill my enemy tonight. He promises that we will both die. This brings such a sly and aching smile to my soul. I can't wait to die in the arms of my enemy. I took steep bribes and gave dark favors but I have finally got my hands on everything I need. Master said everything would be provided if I was truly willing to pay any price to see my enemy fall. I paid every price asked of me. I gave of my body and I gave of my blood and now the night has come. Thunder through the darkened sky and I imagine white cracks in the void above this concrete and steel cage. Thunder – just the same as the night my enemy put me in here… the same night my Master came to me. Now I can hear explosions in the sky, and in the halls outside this small block where solitary confinement lies, I can hear the cries of a thousand convicts a'riot as the face of Officer Lemon appears in the small window at my cell-door.

Master says "It's time child. He comes to die with you."

"Yes Master" I reply as I set fire to the mattress and pillow in a pile under that window.

I can feel the blade in my hand – same as I can feel it ache to enter my foe. The white stark loop of the noose I made for my own neck finds a perfect frame of Officer Lemon's face as he is shouting through the now opening door. I can't make out his words under my Master's voice laughing and yelling "kill him! Kill him!"

"Yes Master" I say as I slip my neck into the noose and step from the bunk.

It takes my enemy just as long as Master said it would to reach me tumbling over the piled flames, and just as Master said would happen – my enemy begins to try to lift me from my noose – exposing his neck to my bladed hand.

Silence in the smoke.

"Now."

"Yes Master." I repeat in my mind for the last time as I grip the blade tightly.

<u>The Prose of Zak Reinhart</u>

The fear of expressing my true self

How many times I have abandoned myself
at the gates of this fear.

All the feelings I felt but held inside.

Afraid to say what I truly feel when the
opportunity is staring at me right in the face
as all the doubt that preludes my life creeps
over me.

Nobody taught me how to express myself
and after a lifetime of trial and error it
seems i have accumulated every fear in the
book of emotional vulnerability.

Choosing ambiguity at the cost of forfeiting
every amazing opportunity ever given to
me.

Playing life with a passiveness that keeps all
potential a safe distance away.

Just so I can escape the judgment of others.

Just so I wont be humiliated by their rejection.

Just so I won't be misunderstood.

Just so my vulnerability can't be manipulated.

Just so I can avoid loosing you from the confrontation.

Just to not reinforce my unworthiness of love once my brokenness scares them away.

Just because I feel powerless to express the complexity of feelings I have.

Always doubting the possibility that what I feel is valid; and that it can be understood or even reciprocated.

Doubting that good things can even happen to me.

Choosing to run and hide behind the excuses that always prevent good things from happening.

With this comes the realization of how much life I have missed by keeping myself stifled and hiding my true feelings from the world.

Stories that never came to be because I was afraid to take a chance to try to make it happen.

Haunting me like the ghosts of my past who know things that I'll never know. Moaning their imperceptible wisdom from behind the barriers of lifetimes I'll never live.

So many opportunities that the weight of regret could crush my bones to dust.

The Deadheads Transition To The Afterlife

by Mila Womb, Investigative Reporter

On a beautiful summer day in Boulder, thousands upon thousands of crusty stale hippies descended upon the city, leaving behind their cabins, shacks, and reserved mobile home parking spots to make the treacherous journey to come face to face with their maker, their holy lord, their God of Gods: The Grateful Dead (or what's left of them anyway).

I stepped outside my new apartment in Goss Grove when the smell of dandelions and musty armpit sweat wafted almost sweetly into my nostrils. 'I've smelled this before', I thought to myself.

I followed the scent a few blocks toward downtown Boulder. Flashes of an adventure in San Francisco's Golden Gate

Park began to flood my mind. An adventure kickstarted by some friendly hippies that had offered me and my friend some acid gummies.

They had the same smell.

Could it be them?

I turned the corner onto Arapahoe, and was engulfed into a sea of people wearing tie dye clothing. In that instant I nearly regurgitated the gluten-free waffle that my roommate had made for breakfast.

This happened largely because I'm allergic to gluten-free food, but let's blame it on the swirls of colorful patterns that disorient onlookers as if by design.

I felt a hand on my shoulder and shivered. I spun about to see a pair of bare feet and a grinning octogenarian with a polaroid. "Hey now friend, could you take our picture?"

"No," I said and tapped my press pass. "Not in the job description."

His smile fell to a frown.

I took the picture.

I did a quick google search: old white

people + Boulder + tie dye + July 1. An article read "Dead and Company's final tour".

Like any good underemployed and overeducated Boulderite would, I decided to investigate.

As I roamed through Goss Grove, it became clear that the neighborhood had turned into a holy campsite.

Worshippers wearing the garbs of the priestly class (mostly tie-dye and shirts with dancing bears and pot leaves on them) flocked the streets in droves. It reminded me of Hajj, a pilgrimage to Mecca that Muslims are required to make once in their lifetime.

These worshippers go by the name Deadheads, and they too, have traveled from distant lands for this special ceremony.

But they brought their mobile homes and their entire families. Also, a fee of $185 - $800 is required to enter this ceremony. And that doesn't even include the cost of the sacred garments that must be worn to participate in the ritual. And for many of them, they have made this expensive journey more than once.

The purpose of Hajj is to cleanse your soul of worldly sins. I spoke with one of the elder worshippers, Richard Dake, 88, who's been to over 100 shows. His soul appeared spotless and his conscious clear as whistle, but his body was breaking down. He was walking around with an oxygen tank due to a lung disease. I asked Dake very directly, "Why are you here?" His response is something that has deeply moved me and stuck with me in the subsequent weeks: "I'm just here to do shrooms and have a good time before I kick the bucket."

I found myself in the center of Shakedown Street, a flea market for their religious products. A thriving economy for those who have rejected American society.

People were walking around yelling "Mushrooms for sale!" like it was hot dogs at a baseball game.

I purchased some to support the cause.

I made eye contact with a beautiful woman wearing a flowy dress and sat next to her in a field of grass. "I can't believe this it, I don't know where my life will go after this weekend, but it's been a hell of a ride," said Cassandra Waterton, 74, as she performed cat cow yoga movements, preparing her soul for the first night of sacred ritual. Her hair was filled with white dandelions and what appeared to be fleas.

But it was coming to an end. This is likely the band's final sermon in Boulder, their sermon on the rock.

Waterton left her cottage in Durango, Colorado a week before and began hitchhiking to see the group's last ceremony in Boulder.

She told me that her life has revolved around this community of music and magic. It was her north star, her guiding light, the sun to her earth. This community has carried her through the chaos of American society. "If it wasn't for the Dead, I don't think I'd be alive, "she said.

This band, and these people had provided her with a way of life that included both "real freedom" as well as something maybe even more transcendent.

"Quality orgies." she smiled and nodded her head in satisfaction.

The band changed their name from the Grateful Dead after the founding prophet Jerry Garcia passed away in 1995. "Things haven't been the same since Jerry crossed over, but his message was so powerful, that we must continue to spread his words... we must.", Waterton preached as tears ran down her face.

If Jerry is the guy who inspired the Cherry Garcia ice cream flavor then I owe him a great debt. That flavor helped me through many weekends of high school while scrolling through social media feeds and watching my classmates do fun things while I sat in my room and ate from 2 pints simultaneously to keep me from the existential abyss of adolescence in a bourgeois society.

Maybe I would be skinnier, but being skinny is not even not cool anymore, so whatever.

The 3-night ceremony of music and light was held at the sacred communal ground of Folsom Field. It is the same ground where savage gladiators battle and hurl themselves at each other while running full speed and carrying a piece of leather on Sunday in a much different kind of ceremony American Football. It's both a place where games are held in honor of a god called Capitalism.

At first I was angry to see these old hippies frolicking through town with smiles and carefree abandon, but after some time in their company, it became clear that their message was one of relentless peace.

"Nothin left to do but smile smile smile" people kept repeating like a holy mantra. I caught myself whispering it in moments of rest and often smiling myself. (A shameful performance for a nihilist, really)

But I couldn't deny, their scriptures were potent antidotes for my depression. I also received many blessings from strangers. It was clear that none of them could harm anything or anyone, except maybe your chances of having a stable income. So I decided to ignore all the empty IPA cans and veritable haze of marijuana that floated around town like some cartoon cloud.

To get more insight into their holy scriptures I mingled into a group of worshippers outside the entrance gate before the ceremony; here is where I met James Greenballs and Blue Owl. They met in San Francisco during the one of the band's first ceremonies in 1967. I was told, rather emphatically, that this is where they took LSD and experienced the 'true meaning of life'.

They've been following the group on every tour in their motor home ever since. Blue Owl said that she committed to taking LSD once a month in honor of their transcendent experience and as a form of prayer to most high Jerry Garcia. "So what's the meaning of life?", I asked. "To love everyone like we love Jerry."

I stood near a dance circle that broke out in the middle of the street. I was amazed at how these worshippers danced and frolicked in public with absolute freedom.

"At some point you just stop caring and let go" said Greenballs.

I had a hard time letting go and moving the way they did. I care way too much about what people think.

How would I be if I didn't care?

As the show began, I watched a family of four walk up to the entry gate. A father carried a baby in a chest sling, with a wife and a boy at his side. The mother stopped and looked directly into the father's eyes. It felt like an eternity. They were eye gazing for what must have been about 5 minutes. Then they both stuck out their tongues. They simultaneously placed a dried mushroom into one another's mouths, closed their eyes, bowed their heads, and walked inside.

I spotted Richard Dake outside of the gate laying down on the lawn alone. I was concerned because he did not have his oxygen tank with him so I went over to check on him. I asked him if he was okay and if needed any help getting inside for the ceremony.

"This is it", he softly muttered, "It's happening".

"What's happening?", I quickly asked.

He appeared to take his final

breathe, "Nothin left to do but...". He was gone.

"Smile, smile, smile" I whispered.

A minute later he opened his eyes, very much alive.

"I'm totally stoned, man."

Thank You For Reading!

If you're interested in more check out our website

www.thewheelart.com

and follow us on Instagram and Substack

@Thewheelart_

https://thewheelcollective.substack.com/